J Parlane

Notes on the Scots' Darien Expedition

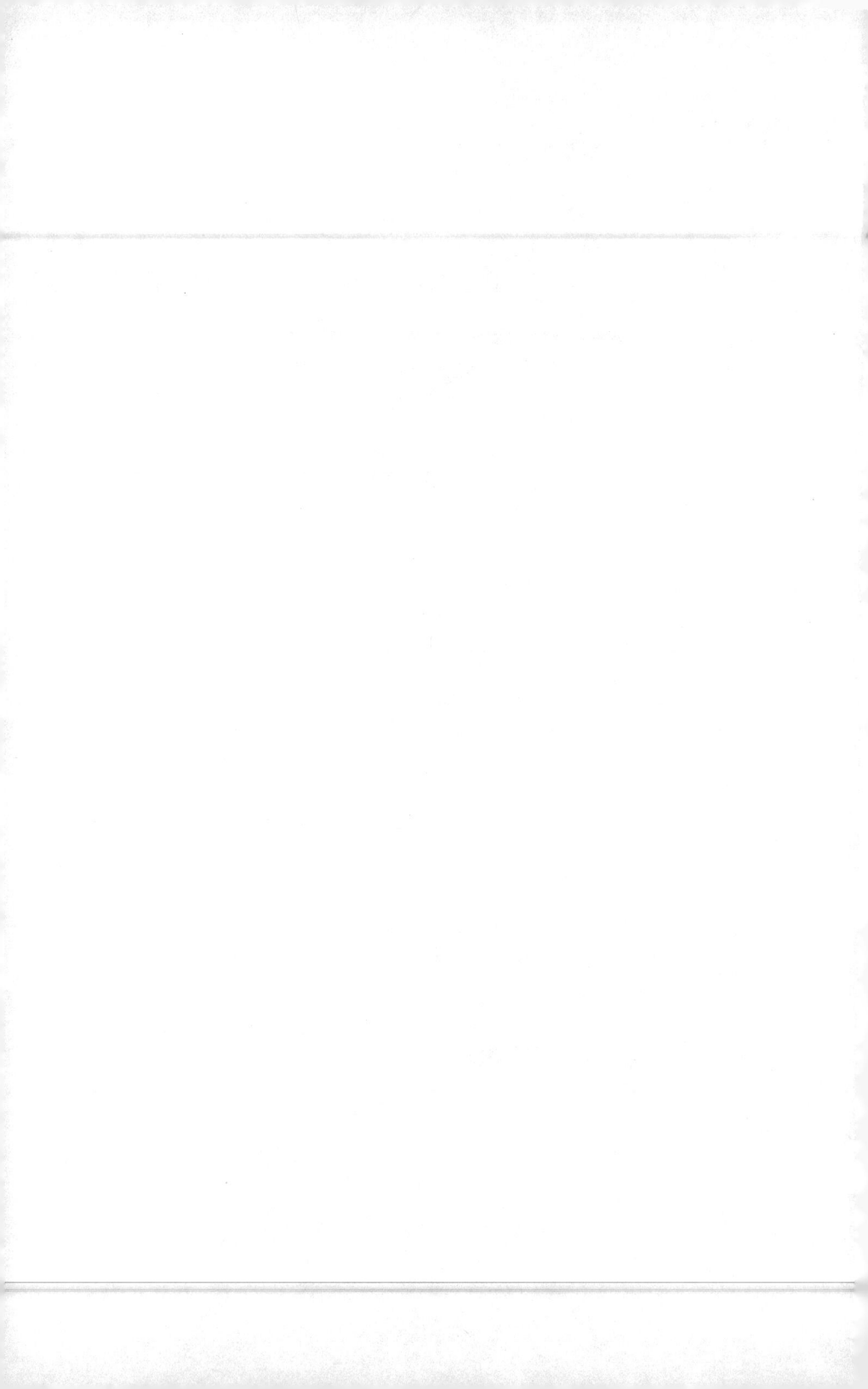

J Parlane

Notes on the Scots' Darien Expedition

ISBN/EAN: 9783337324261

Printed in Europe, USA, Canada, Australia, Japan

Cover: Foto ©Andreas Hilbeck / pixelio.de

More available books at **www.hansebooks.com**

NOTES

ON THE

Scots' Darien Expedition.

Taken from Books and contemporary Pamphlets
in my possession.

JUNE 1888.

J. P.

MANCHESTER:

PALMER AND HOWE, 73, 75, & 77, PRINCESS STREET.

1888.

PREFACE.

———◆———

These Notes have been compiled without any reference whatever to present politics in the United Kingdom ; nor have they any relation to the Panama Canal scheme, which is of such vital importance to France. Everyone reading them must be struck with the fact that the failure of the Darien scheme, two centuries ago, shewed that the union of England and Scotland was an absolute necessity. Who knows but that the possible financial failure of the present Panama Canal Company may have an equally potent and unexpected influence on French politics ? The infatuation of the French investing tradesmen seems to have been, of late years, as complete as was that of the Scotch burghers and gentry of 1696, and failure may be productive of equally momentous results. In the case of England and Scotland, the result was for the good of the two nations and of the world; and it is to be hoped, that whatever is the result of the Panama scheme, both France and the world may be advantaged in the end.

NOTES

ON THE

Scots' Darien Expedition.

FOR a long period before the close of the seventeenth century, the history of Scotland had been chiefly connected with struggles relating to religion and church government. The persecutions in connection with Laud in the reign of Charles I., and afterwards in the time of Charles II., had absorbed a good deal of the energy of the nation, and had overshadowed most other subjects. The social condition of Scotland at the end of the seventeenth century was very bad indeed: beggary prevailed to an extent that would now be thought incredible; trade was in a most backward condition, and agriculture was no less unstudied and neglected. The nation had always been a restless one. I do not speak of the Celtic or Gaelic speaking populations of the West and North-

B

west, who were restless in their own way, and were
ever warring against each other, clan against clan,
varied by predatory incursions into the Eastern and
Central districts—

> " Wrenching from ruin'd Lowland swain,
> IIis herds and harvests rear'd in vain."

At the end of the seventeenth century the Celtic
part of Scotland had hardly begun to be of interest
in the development of the nation, and its position
with regard to the world was quite an unknown
quantity.

The Border forays had long before been forgotten;
the feudal retainers of the Border chiefs had been
disbanded, and almost all trace of their power had
disappeared. The Continent had, not long before,
been an outlet for a certain amount of the energy of
the English-speaking portion of the nation: witness
the Life Guards of France and the regiments of
Gustavus Adolphus. The Scotch Life or Body-
guard of the French Kings was continued after the
exploits of Joan of Arc, which had been greatly
assisted by thousands of Scotch soldiers, headed by
members of the best families of their native land.
The first mention made of the Scottish Archers as
a body-guard of the Kings of France is in 1425,
and for three hundred years they served their post
with unflinching fidelity. In the account of this
body-guard, most elaborately written a few years
since by William Forbes-Leith, of the S.J., the

muster-rolls of the men-at-arms are given for almost every year, and the French spelling of familiar Scotch names is often very amusing. The writer prefaces his volume with an extract from Claude Seysul, Master of Requests to Louis XII., to the effect "that so long a time as they have served in France, never hath there been one of them found that hath committed any fault against the kings and their state;" and this character they maintained to the end. The number of Scotch soldiers employed in the seventeenth century by France, and previously in the fifteenth and sixteenth centuries, is incredible to any who have not looked up the authorities on the subject; and the numbers who fought in the same century, first of all attracted by the cause of the Elector Palatine—the husband of the daughter of James I. of Scotland—is no less astonishing. These regiments, or their successors, ultimately found their way to fight under the banners of Mansfield; afterwards they assisted the Dutch, and then passed into the hands of the King of Denmark. At last, as the late Dr. Burton says in his "Scot Abroad," they found their true master in Gustavus Adolphus, who knew their qualities, and made full use of them in building up the great fabric of his fame. In the well-known "Memoirs and Adventures of Sir John Hepburn," by Grant, thirteen regiments of Scottish infantry are enumerated as being in the service of Gustavus Adolphus, and many corps of pikemen in

his service were officered by Scotchmen; and after
an enumeration of them by Sir Thomas Urquhart
and Colonel Alex. Hamilton, the latter says that
immediately after the battle of Leipsic, in one place
and at one time, he had thirty-six Scottish colonels
about him.

Not only did they find an outlet for their energies
in the armies of Europe, but they overran the North
of Europe with their packs of merchandise. The
Baltic towns and villages swarmed with them, and
numbers traded through Germany and into the heart
of Poland.

As the seventeenth century approached its close,
the religious persecutions and troubles of the country
had been practically put an end to. The Revolution
of 1688, and the accession of William and Mary, made
all classes in the Lowlands, and more particularly
the townsfolk, think that they were entering on a
period of prosperity. The king, as is well known,
was "very indifferent to Scotland and to Scotch
affairs," and no stronger proof of this need be given
than his conduct in connection with the Glencoe
Massacre and the Panama or Darien Scheme, which
latter I am going to describe. Fortunately for the
peace of Scotland, and for its escape from what
might have been fatal mistakes as regards its future,
the king allowed himself to be guided in all Scotch
affairs by his chaplain, William Carstairs, excepting
where high policy as regards the relation of Great

Britain to the state of Europe was concerned. Carstairs accompanied the king from Holland, was confirmed in his appointment of court chaplain, residing generally in Edinburgh, and filling in addition the charge of Greyfriars, and afterwards of St. Giles, in that city. He was also principal of the University, and was chosen four times to be the moderator of the General Assembly. His influence with William was almost complete, and it was always used for what has turned out for the good of his native land. His influence was still considerable in the following reign, but he unsuccessfully opposed measures regarding church patronage which were carried, and which subsequent experience has proved were national mistakes. The country had until this point derived very little benefit from the union of the two crowns in 1603, though great things in the way of national aggrandisement were expected from that event at the time. Treaties of commerce were drawn up making trade between the countries free, and the English judges declared that Scotchmen born after the Union were not aliens. Scotland only, however, derived full benefit from the Union in the short-lived reign of Cromwell, and on the return of Charles II., in an act for encouraging shipping, Scotchmen were classed as aliens, and it was enacted that no goods could be exported or imported out of Asia, Africa, or America but in English or Irish bottoms, or in vessels of those plantations, and in all these vessels three-fourths of the mariners were to be English. The more effectually to exclude Scotch ships, it was enacted that by "English ships" was meant ships built in England, Ireland, Wales, Jersey, Guernsey, Berwick-on-Tweed, or in any of the lands of His Majesty in Africa, Asia, or America. No ships but such as were English built and manned could trade in the country-trade of England and Ireland, and no product of the English plantations was allowed to be imported into Scotland direct. All traffic by land from Scotland to England had to pass either through Carlisle or Berwick, and to submit to taxation. The literature of the time shews that the people felt that they had all the inconveniences of the Union and none of the advantages they had expected to derive from it.

After 1688, the country having calmed and settled down in the absence of political disturbing causes, Scotchmen turned their energies into another direction. They remembered the advantages they had enjoyed during the short-lived commonwealth, and an overpowering desire for material advancement by trade seized the nation, and numerous schemes and suggestions for advancing *the interest of Scotland* were broached. In a small book in my library, published about this time, and entitled "Ways and Means for making the Nation a Gainer in Foreign Commerce," the writer takes for a motto *Proverbs* xii. 24—"The hand of the diligent shall bear rule, but the slothful

shall be under tribute." The writer, after describing
what Scotch trade might have been, considering
that the Scotch nation's relation to foreign princes
and powers was so much more favourable than
that of England—instancing "in politics Scotland's
friendship with Spain, and the special privileges
enjoyed by Scotchmen in France, and the fact that
Scottish fisheries ought really to have brought the
nation into contact with the Catholic nations of
Europe,"—further shews how the Scotch Privy
Council were powerless to advance Scotch interests
whenever they were in any way detrimental to
English. He says also: "When we were under
a distinct head from that of England, the English,
wanting a security that we would make no offensive
alliance with their enemies, were desirous to oblige
us on all occasions, but as soon as they got us under
the same sovereign, they have taken care, notwithstanding the divisions at home, to crush such of our
national attempts at commerce which have had the
least appearance of clashing with theirs."

One of the most interesting chapters in Scottish
history relates to the great commercial scheme
which took hold of the national mind at this time,
and, in the end, was mainly the cause which made
the union of the two nations necessary and possible.
The moving spirit in this enterprise was William
Paterson, a great and successful enthusiast, who,
from a combination of circumstances, managed to

become the national hero, and, at this particular time, wielded immense influence. Writing of the year 1694 and of the establishment of the Bank of England in that year, Macaulay says : "All the projectors of that time were not absurd. One of them, William Paterson, was an ingenious though not a judicious speculator. Of his early life little is known except that he was a native of Scotland, and had been in the West Indies. In what character he had visited the West Indies was a matter about which opinions differed. His friends said that he had been a missionary ; his enemies that he had been a buccaneer. He seems to have been gifted by nature with fertile invention, an ardent temperament and great powers of persuasion, and to have acquired somewhere in the course of his vagrant life a perfect knowledge of accounts." Paterson's scheme for establishing the Bank of England lay in abeyance for three years before it was taken up by the London merchants, and, from urgent financial considerations, supported by the government. When so taken up in 1694 the result was the Bank of England more or less as it now exists.

Paterson's restless mind did not allow him to remain long idle, and he found the Scottish nation in the nervously unsettled state I have described, and ready to lend a willing ear to, and to meet more than half-way, the plausible and persuasive projector who came with the prestige derived from his late banking success.

In 1695, the first Scotch parliament of King William, in its fifth session, passed an Act for the Encouragement of Foreign Trade, and in the same session an act of incorporation was granted to the Company of Scotland trading to Africa and the Indies. *The interest of Scotland* was the main purpose of the undertaking, and one of the conditions of the grant was that at least half of the stock was to be held by Scotchmen residing in Scotland, and that inalienably. The remaining half was to be allotted to Scotchmen residing either in Scotland or else-where, or to foreigners. Many favourable conditions were granted to the company, and its officers were empowered to plant colonies in any parts of Asia, Africa, or America which were not possessed by any European power, and to which possession the natives did not object. The ships were to return with their cargoes to Scotland, without breaking bulk, on pain of forfeiture, and the company was to have the sole right of trading from Scotland to these three quarters of the globe, right of seizure and forfeiture being granted against all delinquents. By way of acknow-ledgment, the company was to pay to the crown yearly, if required, a hogshead of tobacco. The company was empowered to have a common seal, and the concession was to hold good for thirty-one years from the 31st August 1696.

One of the first letters written by Paterson from London to the Lord Provost of Edinburgh, who was one of a dozen names mentioned in the Act of Concession, shews a great deal of worldly wisdom. He suggests, with the consent of the Scotchmen in London, also named therein, that the first meeting should be in that city, and that the grant should be kept secret for a time, lest that the English parliament should take alarm at the concessions made to the company. Besides, he says, "as the Scotch parliament had given the Kingdom of Scotland twelve months' time to subscribe for half the stock, it was unwise to appear before the public till within three or four months of that time." "And for that we have many instances here in England, where, when the parliament gives a long day for money, that fund has hardly ever success; and where the days are short, they seldom ever fail. The Bank of England had but six weeks' time from the opening of the bookes, and was finished in nine dayes; and in all subscriptions here it is limited to a single day; for if a thing goe not with the first heat, the raising of a fund seldom or never succeeds, the multitude being comonly ledd more by example than reason." Paterson concludes by asserting that there were many harbingers of success, and expresses the hope that the Almighty would bless their endeavour, and "make some use of Scotland to visit the dark places of the earth, whose habitations are full of cruelty."

The historian, John H. Burton, when preparing his History of Scotland, searching in the Advocates'

Library, Edinburgh, for information regarding the history of the country before and at the time of the Union, had occasion to overhaul a collection of books and loose papers relating to the company commonly called the Darien Company. He thought them so interesting that he communicated the gist of their contents to the well-known Bannatyne Club, and at a meeting of the club committee in 1848, it was resolved that a volume of these original letters and papers should be selected and edited by Mr. Burton, and printed for the members of the club. The result is the very handsome quarto volume called " The Darien Papers," published in the following year.

This volume contains minutes and abstracts of proceedings, and a mass of general correspondence is also preserved in it. It shews, from the confusion in its chronological sequence, how involved the correspondence was, and how, owing to the irregular and delayed communication, the affairs in Darien were unknown in Scotland, and how the mistakes at home and in the colony produced fatal results which more speedy communication might have rectified or prevented.

The papers and books preserved are models of correctness, and the book-keeping could not be now improved on. The minutes of the board meetings were evidently most faithfully kept, and Dr. Burton records with what interest he took "from their long rest these mute and methodical memorials of an

incident connected with so much excitement and
suffering—with the exultations of a whole people."
He notes the neat and systematic order of these
records, their fresh, business-like appearance, and
"their perfect similarity to those volumes which, in
the present day, are methodically removed from the
office-safe, laid on the mahogany desk, and turned
over by individuals throned on three-legged stools.
The journals and ledgers, many of them of gigantic
size, would excite no passing remark on their obsolete
appearance if they were seen lying open, with the
ink wet, on a bank-counter of the present day." He
adds : "Some of the larger volumes have over the
regular binding a loose cover of soft red leather,
of the sort still used to mitigate the wear and tear of
books requiring to be regularly handled." The
accounts were all kept in sterling money. "The
writing is clear and distinct, and would, at the
present day, be called the perfection of bank clerk
caligraphy."

Half of the original capital was reserved, as has
been mentioned, for Scotland ; the other half was at
once subscribed in England ; but the whole strength
of the London merchants and the House of Commons
was brought to bear against the undertaking. The
English East India Company and the English
African Company sank their animosity and rivalry,
and joined to make common cause against the
interloping company ; the books of the new company

were seized, and though they had acted under an act of the Scots' parliament, the directors in Scotland were ordered to be impeached of high crimes and misdemeanours! This insulting denunciation, while it stopped the English subscribers from implementing their undertaking as regards payment of the first call (excepting as regards five directors including Paterson, who had put down their names for £3,000 sterling each), had the effect of rousing the pride of the Scotch nation to such a pitch, that not only did they subscribe for their quota of £300,000, but for a further sum of £100,000. The nation felt the sting of poverty which had been cast in their teeth by the rich English traders, and "they resolved to shew the world that Scotland was neither so poor nor so disjointed as some people would have it believed." The Hamburg merchants had resolved at one time to take stock to the amount of £100,000, but great pressure was brought on them to withdraw their support, and the English Minister to that republic, Sir Paul Rycaut, was instructed to support these representations, and the result, as given in the "History of Caledonia by a Gentleman lately arrived," published in 1699 and described later on, "was that the Humburgher at last resolved to desist, preferring certain riches" (meaning English trade) "before uncertain gain."

The subscribers to the scheme were thoroughly representative of all classes of the nation, save, significantly, of the Highlands, which seemed to be only represented by some trifling subscriptions from some of the small traders in Inverness. Subscribers with the prefix of "Mac" are almost absent from the list, and such as do appear on it are almost invariably those with such names as are peculiar to Ayrshire and Galloway.

The list of subscribers was headed by the Duchess of Hamilton and Chastelrault, whose name appears for £3,000, and several of the nobility appear for like amounts: the Duke of Argyll for £1,500; the provosts of Edinburgh and Glasgow, for their corporations, for £3,000 each; and the gentry, the clergy, lawyers, and traders generally, for amounts which shew the national interest in the undertaking. The total sum subscribed by 1,400 subscribers was £400,000, and the total sum actually paid up from first to last was £219,094, a sum which Macaulay describes as "marvellous," and greater, considering the poverty of the country, than any voluntary contribution that any other nation ever made for a commercial undertaking. He estimates that the relative importance of the sum paid up would only be equalled by one hundred times the amount at the present time, taking the wealth of Scotland into account.

The minutes of the proceedings of the Court of Directors were carefully kept, and, theoretically, all the steps taken were such as would have ensured success; but when the practical application came, the scheme was found to be visionary and ill-considered, and without any direction from a head with a clear perception of the means to be adopted to meet the end in view, the whole affair from beginning to end being a curious compound of genius and imbecility, grand ideas, indefinite aims, and random management. A resolution was passed at an early meeting appointing special directors to negotiate all the company's affairs beyond the seas, and the secretary was instructed to translate the same into Latin. Sub-committees were appointed. Two houses in Mill's Square, Edinburgh, were bought for the company's warehouse at a cost of about £850. Salaries were fixed for clerks and others, and even the hours of attendance were carefully minuted. It is interesting to note that the regular office-hours were fixed at from 8 to 12 in the forenoon, and from 2 to 6 in the afternoon. The cash was to be balanced every night, and regulations regarding the lending money to subscribers on the amount of their subscriptions were passed, along with many other regulations now in force with joint-stock companies registered according to modern acts of parliament.

The salaries were by no means extravagant according to our modern notions, but no doubt, according to the Scotch standard of two hundred years ago, they were sufficiently liberal. The secretary received £150 per annum, the chief accountant and the chief cashier received respectively £120, and the assistants from £25 to £70 each.

My impression is that to the word *director* the Darien Company attached something more of the French than the English meaning. The Scotch took many of their ideas from the French, as is well known, and the French, nowadays at any rate, understand by *director*, as a rule, what we would define by the word *manager*. At any rate, the directors entered into the minutiæ of management, instead of confining themselves to general policy. They seem to have met earlier than do boards of management nowadays, as, according to the minutes, they usually met at 9 a.m., and even at 7 a.m. The minutiæ of their management may be imagined by such an entry as the following in the minutes: "Upon a representation from Mr. Herries, purser of the 'Caledonia,' that he wanted flour for pudding, and that the use of pudding would save so much beef; ordered Ninian Hay, the company's baker, to deliver to him, upon his receipt, twelve stone of flour."

This ship, the "Caledonia," was the first vessel purchased for the expedition, and on the 20th August 1697, instructions were given to Captain William Tennant to proceed to Hamburg, where she was laying, to take command of her. Another vessel called the "Instauration," commanded by

Captain John Brown, was also at Hamburg, and the two vessels were directed to return to Leith under the convoy of His Majesty's ship, the "Royal William." Letters of marque were granted by the Scots' privy council to the "Caledonia," as also to the "Instauration," to Robert Pinkerton, captain of the "Union," and James Gibson, captain of the "Rising Sun."

For the government of the colony a council was appointed, and "fundamental constitutions as a perpetual rule of government for the colony" were resolved on.

The regulations were very minute. Liberty to trade in the colony which was to be founded was to be free to all. The company reserved to themselves one-twentieth of all lands and one-twentieth of all gold dust, mines of silver, and pearl fishing. All goods imported into the colony in Scotch ships were, after 1702, to pay 2 per cent duty, in other ships 3 per cent, but if from America and the produce of America, 1 per cent duty only. An export duty of from 2 to 4 per cent was also ordered.

The regulations and mode of trading were most concise, and the way the colony was to recoup the company is laid down very clearly. The council consisted of Major James Cunningham, Mr. James Montgomery, Mr. Daniel Mackay, Capt. Robert Jolly, Capt. Robert Pennicuik, Capt. William Vetch, and Capt. Robert Pinkerton; and one of

c

their first instructions was, that on arriving at the point indicated in their sailing instructions, they were to land and take possession of the place in the company's name, holding it of the crown of Scotland. Accurate accounts were to be kept, and also full minutes of their proceedings, which were to be sent home in duplicate. All inns and drinking-houses were to be at the disposal of the local government towards the expense thereof. In the "Darien Papers," published by the Bannatyne Club, there are very full particulars given of the goods ordered for the cargoes of the ships. They consisted largely of iron work, axes, wedges and knives, nails, carpenters' tools, guns, tobacco-pipes, fish-hooks, and horn-spoons. Fifty pounds sterling was paid to Agnes Campbell, relict of Andrew Anderson, printer, in advance of a "bargan" of Bibles and Catechisms. Linen and woollen goods were purchased under descriptions not now common; and from Jeromie Robertson, periwig-maker in Edinburgh, 25 campaign wigs at 15s. each, and 25 bob wigs at 6s. each, were ordered.

On the 6th December 1696, the committee ordered 610 ells of Stirling serges, to be delivered to John Pringle, dyer, in Edinburgh. These 610 ells were the lengths of fourteen pieces. He was also to receive for dyeing blue the same length of linen cloth. The colours for the serges were to be fixed at the next meeting of the committee, when the cost of dyeing was also to be considered. Five days later the committee again met, when it was unanimously resolved that one-fourth should be dyed black, one-fourth blue, one-fourth of assorted reds, and one-fourth of several sorts of cloth colours.

All being ready, the first expedition sailed from Leith about the end of July 1698, the number of colonists and seamen being about 1,200. A very good account of the progress made is preserved in the journal of Mr. Hugh Rose, and published by the Bannatyne Club, which shews the vague idea which the colonists seem to have had of their destination, or of what they were to do when they reached it; other correspondence published by the same society also confirms this; but apart from these, the literature of the last three or four years of the seventeenth century, and the first few years of the eighteenth century, is full of the Darien Company, and the collection of books written on the subject is very worthy of study. I happen to have a good number of these books and pamphlets, collected as opportunity offered during the last six or seven years, and have found the perusal of them very interesting. All shew the hold the scheme had on the national mind, and the unwillingness of the nation to believe that it was chimerical, and under the circumstances impracticable. There runs also through many of them a combination of shrewdness and simplicity, intense interest in the colonists themselves, and a combination also of kindly interest in the natives of the countries they meant to possess, and a desire to further the Christian religion as far as it was in accordance with the ideas of the Presbyterian Church of Scotland.

One pamphlet in my collection is entitled : " A Letter from the Commission of the General Assembly of the Church of Scotland, met at Glasgow, 21st July 1699, to the Honourable Council and Inhabitants of the Scots' Colony of *Caledonia* in America." The letter begins with the prayer that grace, mercy, and peace may be multiplied unto them, and assures them that " though, through the Providence of God, they were separated from them, yet were they not disjointed from their hearts, nor shall these waters ever quench, nor time, nor distance wear out our love."

After acknowledging the special mercies vouch-safed in the starting of such a great undertaking by a poor nation unacquainted with trade, the letter continues its acknowledgment that the first noble adventurers have been led out of their own country under divine direction to a land which the Lord had " espyed and reserved," and " to which he had borne them as on eagles' wings, and piloted them safely to that void but commodious dwelling to which, like Abraham who knew not whither he went, they had gone." The letter mentions with grief the having heard the news that the Rev. Mr. Thomas

James had died in the passage, and the Rev. Mr. Adam Scott shortly after landing, of what, in the official return made to the company, is called "the flux." The commission promise to accede to the adventurers' request to send out four other members, who are to form a church-court with the assistance of elders, and for these ministers the commissioners "pray that they may be highly esteemed in love for their works' sake ; that their hands may be strengthened and their endeavours encouraged." The whole letter shews most touching solicitude for the welfare, temporal and spiritual, of the colonists, and though couched in quaint language with texts of Scripture somewhat needlessly inserted after the fashion of the time, no one can read it without feeling that the heart of the writers was wrapped up in their subject, and that love like that of a mother inspired every line. The colonists are reminded that the eyes of God, of angels, and of men are on them, and they are besought "for the Lord's sake, for their own souls' sake, and for the sake of their country and their own posterity, and for the interest of the commonwealth and for all that ought to be sacred, to live honest lives, abhorring uncleanness, idleness, falsehood, and unjust dealings." They are exhorted to be just and honest towards the natives, "shewing them obliging kindness," so that they, "beholding and enjoying the benefits of your good works may glorifie God in the day of your visitation. If you partake of their temporal things, are you not bound to minister unto them of your spiritual things?" Idleness is spoken of as being the parent of mischief and beggary, and the colonists are warned against letting the foolish notion get hold of them which has been one great cause of the poverty of their nation at home, and their reproach among the rich and trading nations abroad, *that it is below a gentleman to follow trade and employment.* The colonists are enjoined to pay submission and dutiful deference to their rulers ; to bear with patience and contentment the toil and fatigue of the first settlement, " not murmuring for what uneasiness may as yet be in your circumstances, but waiting on the Lord in an humble and diligent application to your present work, till He in His mercy give you a confirmed rest in the Lord; for though you do not find such fruits attending your present labours as may answer your expectations, yet patience, diligence, and industry will overcome your first difficulties, and through the blessing of God, you shall find the promise made out to you that the *hand of the diligent maketh rich.*"

In the very interesting small book published in 1699, entitled "The History of Caledonia; or, The Scots' Colony of Darien. By a Gentleman lately Arrived" (*i.e.* returned), the writer describes the country as being "the most famous isthmus in the world." "It is about 120 miles long and 60 broad. If it were possible [he says] to cut a channel from

sea to sea, capable of shipping, it would facilitate
the navigation of the world two parts in three, but
it is next to an impossibility, for it is almost a
continued chain of mountains, of which some are as
high as any of the Alps. The valleys are watered
with rivers and perpetual clear streams, which are
most pleasant to drink, as soft as milk and very
nourishing. The hills are clothed with tall trees
without any underwood, so that one may gallop
conveniently among them many miles from sun and
river unless of a great continuance. The air makes
in the tops of the trees a pleasant melancholy
musick, so that one of the colony, considering the
coolness, pleasant murmuring of the air, and the
infinite beauty of a continued natural arbor, called
them the Shades of Love." The writer also
describes the mines of gold, and the mineral wealth
of the country. He describes the first interview
which some deputies, accompanied by Mr. Paterson,
had with the Indians, whom they impressed with
the idea that they would not, like the Spaniards,
interfere with their religion. The Indians are
described as being tall and clean-limbed, with
straight, long black hair, to which the use of a comb
was unknown. They entertained the deputation
with fantastic dances, which reminded them of the
Highland dances in their native land. When they
arrived at the court of the king of the country they
were well received, and mutual vows of assistance

were made. The league was to continue "as long as gold and floods were in Darien," signifying thereby perpetuity. The feasting is described and the entertainment generally; but on the third day they took leave of the king, accompanied by several boys of the native nobility, who were to be educated and taught the Scottish language. The mothers, it is stated, made a very strong protest, but their husbands tried to quieten them by promising them Scotch boys to take their place.

The writer left the country before the disasters began, but he already had some experience of the dangers that were gathering round the infant colony, for he alludes to an engagement in which one hundred Spanish prisoners were taken, who were held as security for the good treatment of Captain Pinkerton, of the "Dolphin," who being forced by distress of weather under the walls of Carthagena, was there made prisoner.

Another writer is "Philo-Caledonius," who was the author of a pamphlet entitled "Scotland's Present Duty, or a Call to the Nobility, Gentry, and Commonality of the Land to be duly affected with, and vigorously to act for, our Common Concern *in Caledonia*, as a means to enlarge Christ's Kingdom, to benefit ourselves, and to do good to all Protestant Churches." The pamphlet was printed in 1700, and in a preface the writer sarcastically says he would "excite all in the land to joyn in an address to the

King of Heaven for help. And this is our comfort, that no courtier there will hinder our address, but rejoice in it, if we approach that Throne with penitent hearts, for the Majesty of Heaven commands us to call upon Him in the day of trouble with penitent hearts and He will hear us."

He divides his address in seven heads as follows :—

1st. We are called to seek the spreading of the gospel and the enlargement of Christ's kingdom.

2nd. Our settlement of Caledonia would be a likely means to that end.

3rd. This design seems to be almost crushed and borne down.

4th. How discouraging this will be to the church and state if the Lord help us not.

5th. What are the procuring sins of this sore and lamentable stroke?

6th. What is now our duty and work with respect to this great concern?

7th. Lastly, there is an invocation to cry to God for help, and to use suitable efforts to retrieve the loss.

These heads are divided into divisions and subdivisions. The second head has very numerous divisions, and though they may be nowadays thought to be hair-splitting, yet they are examples of close and logical reasoning, and are interesting from an antiquarian point of view if from no other.

The first division of the second head says that a new colony of professing Christians might be planted there, who might in turn become a covenanted people, and would proclaim the news of Christ and set up His worship.

The second division of the second head says: " Were once a praying people sent, the colony might become the best in the world ; for 1st, our worship is most pure ; 2nd, our government most adapted to advance the true end of government in God's house beyond what prelacy and independency can pretend to—our discipline (if rightly managed) the most effectual to bear down sin and encourage piety. All these meeting together in the hands of zealous ministers in a new colony must render Zion in that place beautiful as the morning, clear as the sun, fair as the moon, and terrible as an army with banners. 4th, it was a place to which many nations might resort for trade, and to see the comely order of God's house. No. 5 suggests that the colony shall not be confined to Darien, but lengthened as well as their stakes strengthened." The 7th division is further divided into ten sub-divisions, showing that the kindly natives were inclined to them in consequence of their hatred to the Spaniards, and that through trade and the care of their children they would be still further gained over.

Under the other heads the writer strives to stir up the Scots to renew their endeavours to maintain possession of Darien; appealing to their prejudices in every way, to their sense of religion and national honour; and even saying, that in the event of failure the name of Scotsman would become "a bye-word and a jest among the nations, and one almost to be ashamed of."

The writer goes on to enquire why the undertaking had failed so far, and amongst other reasons gives the non-confession of sin, covenant breaking, ingratitude to God for the happy revolution, and neglect of gospel ordinances. The way in which much of the money subscribed had been obtained, and the mode of life of many of the subscribers, are also given as reasons for the failure. The writer calls on the nation "to renew the national covenant, to hold a national fast, and to cry to God who can make crooked things straight, and the mountains a plain before the people." "Who knows," says he, "but that yet He may cause us to sing that song, *Psalm* lxvi., verse 8, to the end?" The whole book is a well-written and closely-argued appeal to the nation, and is a good sample of the mingled simplicity and deep religious feeling of the time, and shews how politics, business, and the national church were interwoven and identified.

A small book entitled " A Defence of the Scotch abdicating Darien, including an Answer, etc.," was published in 1700. The author, in "the Epistle Dedicatory to the Court of Directors of the Scots'

African and Indian Company," says that he is
"emboldened by the great concessions that had
been made to the company by the king," and which
he also describes as "a large and glorious patent,"
to lay an account before them of what he had
actually seen and experienced whilst in the service
of the Darien Company. He says he was the first
person to be employed, and the first to leave the
service; and he writes with a good deal of animus
and sarcasm against the management, and indeed
against the whole undertaking. Though evidently
bitterly prejudiced, there is a good deal of truth in
the book. He tells the directors that if they had
"listened to the advice of Mr. Douglas, an eminent
and experienced man in India, who offered himself
as their security," and "had not been bewitched to
the golden dreams of Paterson the pedlar, tub-
preacher, and at last whimsical projector, they
might ere now have been possessed of a good colony
in India, where nobody could disturb them, and not
have run after an airy project, which (although it
should have met with no opposition from the
Spaniard) four times the Darien capital stock could
not have brought to any reasonable pitch of
answering the end." He also lays great stress on
their silly expenditure on ships in Amsterdam and
Hamburg. Had, instead (he says), "two second-
hand ships been bought in the Thames and
dispatched to India with a suitable cargo (not

Scotch cloth, slippers, periwigs, and Bibles), a very different result might soon have been brought about." But "*Sed quos Deus perdere vult eos dementat,*" he writes when the news of the first abandonment of the colony had reached Scotland, and this came too late, and was only learned by himself by experience of the fallacy of the whole scheme. His arguments are doubtless often correct, but they are not put in a kindly way, and even if they carried conviction, they must have raised a bitter feeling and fanned the national rage. He says: "If you were thus persuaded to run headlong on a blind project at which the trading part of the world stand amazed, the India Companies of England and Holland laugh at in their sleeve, and the rest of mankind admire that people in their right senses should be guilty of; and if the same should miscarry by your own ill management (to say no worse on't), 'tis not fair to snarle at your neighbours who have had no other hand in your misfortune than that they would not be accessory to any act which the world might think felonious, and wherein they could not join without engaging themselves in an unreasonable war, and in the end to assist you with weapons to break their own heads."

He further argues against the outcry for separation by pointing out how that, under King William, they (the Scotch) have stately churches, instead of being accustomed to worship on such altars as

Jacob made; they could (he says) pray either in form or out of form, just as they pleased, without dread of consequences, and their lives and liberties were secure instead of being at the mercy of petty despots and local feuds.

He further excuses the action of the king in the matter; partly by shewing that the whole affair was managed so secretly that the chief news of the undertaking was received when it had collapsed, and what did reach the king's ears some months afterwards was scarcely heard owing to the noise of the Namur guns. "If" (he says) "your colony has left Darien for reasons not as yet made public, 'tis your fault, right worshipful gentlemen, in undertaking to manage a project you so little understood, and not of the English nation, whose interest it is to advance and preserve their own colonies, and to keep them from being rendered desolate by the clandestine artifices of yours. As for this nation entering into a war with the Spaniard on the score of your company, who besides loss in trade must throw away more English pounds thrice over than there are Scotch pounds in your capital stock, I will leave it to any man of half an ounce of politics to find out the jest on't."

The author writes in a very bitter and sarcastic tone of the whole affair, and it is not fair to take his statements without allowing for the animus he continually shews; but subsequent events shew that there is a great deal of truth in his way of stating things. He describes the contract between the company and the council as having been penned before the councillors were created; but that mattered little, as the candidates would have agreed to terms even had they been harder. Seven were appointed, and six more were to be assumed from among such English and French men of substance as should join them in the West India plantations.

He gives the characters at large of these seven councillors, as he says, "in short":—

"1st. James Cunningham led the van; he had been a major in the Scots' forces, and disbanded in the peace; a pillar of the kirk, and never out of Scotland before.

"2nd. Donald Macay, a scrivener's or writer's clerk, newly come out of his apprenticeship. but a youth of good parts.

"3rd. — Veach, a man of no trade, but advanced to this post on the account his father was a godly minister and a glorifier of God, I think in the Grass Market.

"4th. Robert Jollie, a jolly Scotch *ever-grown* Hamburger, who was formerly a skipper, and used the Shetland trade, but had for some dozen years been set up at Hamburg, in the quality of merchant, and after that a broker, and now a councillor.

"5th. Robert Pennycook, formerly a surgeon

in the English navy, then a lieutenant and
afterwards commander of a bomb; this gentleman, having gained experience by being
twenty-one years away from Scotland in various
trades and occupation, was advanced by the
interest of the kirk party, the better to balance
that of the church, and to keep out Dr. M., a
reputed atheist. Mr. Pennycook was not only
councillor, but likewise captain, commodore,
and the very Orford of our navy.

"6th. James Montgomrie, whose designation
I cannot well tell; but you may know him by
the story of the bloody fight he had with the
Spaniard, where so many hundred were taken
prisoners, though at the same time there was
never a Spaniard hurt. This gentleman was
formerly an ensign in the Scots' Guards, but
not liking that office left it, and carried a brown
musket in another regiment, his preferment
being entirely due to influence.

"7th. Robert Pincarton, a good downright,
rough-spun tar; never known before by any
designation or state office save that of boat-
swain to Sir William Phipps, when he was on
the wreck; and now, poor fellow, a diver in
the Spanish mines at Carthagena."

These, says the writer, were the seven wise men
who were to divide Mexico and Peru amongst them.
Veach, being sick of the voyage, stayed at home;

and William Paterson, who had come from Scotland as a volunteer (for he was in disgrace some months before the expedition sailed), was assumed into the senate in Veach's place when the expedition had reached Madeira. Of the ministers on board his ship, he says there were two, "with a journeyman, to take up the psalm." "One minister," he says, "was an extraordinary good man, who owed his education to the army in Flanders;" and the other he describes as "a young headstrong, as infallible as his holiness, saucy, and as impertinent as the moderator himself." Probably the company in which they found themselves had as much effect as the climate on their spirit and health, and despair of the future ill-fitted them for withstanding the disease to which they soon succumbed.

The writer devotes the remainder of his book to considering the Scots' title to settle in the country; and to the *de facto* right of the Spaniard, as shewn by the proximity of Darien to the Spanish ports of Carthagena, Portobello, and Panama, in addition to many smaller towns and garrisons. The names of the Indian captains (such as Andrias), and their knowledge of Spanish customs and language, are given as proofs that the country invaded was under Spanish influence and in Spanish possession.

A very interesting narrative of the Darien Expedition, mainly written in 1700, was published in 1714 in Glasgow. It is written by the Rev. Francis

D

puddle unwholesome water," instead of the river water they were cut off from. As Boreland describes, "what with bad water, salt spoiled provisions, and absence of medicines, the fort was indeed like a hospital of sick and dying men."

In this sad state of matters the Spanish general, Don John Pimienta, "captain of his catholic majestie's forces both by sea and land, and Governor of Carthagena," proposed articles of capitulation, which were agreed to; the articles were drawn up in Latin by one of the colonists who knew French, as did also the Spanish general; but the latter, though he negotiated in French, refused to sign any articles drawn up in French, as being incompatible with his dignity. The Spanish general did not exact hard terms; all he wanted was to get the colonists away as quickly as possible. The guns and most of the ammunition were given up to him, and there was a provision made that any reliefs arriving in the course of two months should be allowed to wood and water, and then depart in peace. An indemnity for the friendly Indians was refused, as the general said they were the King of Spain's subjects, and as such he knew how to deal with them; but he intimated that he would not trouble them if they did not trouble him.

When the colonists surrendered, scarce three hundred were fit for duty, and the deaths were about sixteen men per day. At least three hundred of this last expedition were buried in Caledonia; many died when being taken on board, and the state of the survivors was such that great numbers died of hardship whilst at sea. On the 11th April 1700, the embarkation was completed, and this portion of the expedition, a broken-hearted band, abandoned the country after a stay of only four months and twelve days. The four ships that had come from Scotland in the last expedition, and three others, formed the fleet that left Caledonia, but misfortune after misfortune followed their steps. Malignant fevers and fluxes swept off great numbers, and from the "Rising Sun" alone they would sometimes bury eight in one morning. Mr. Boreland says that on this vessel the sick were crowded together like hogs in a sty, poisoning each other, and with no sustenance but spoiled oatmeal and water. Under such circumstances his services could hardly be rendered, and he mourns his powerlessness. One ship was so leaky that she had to be run into Carthagena, and was there sold to the Spaniards; another was wrecked near to Jamaica, and between Caledonia and Jamaica, in the space of one month, it is supposed that two hundred and fifty men died of disease, and were buried at sea from the different vessels. The "Rising Sun" and several other vessels arrived at length safely in Jamaica, but Captain Campbell's sloop steered for New York, and arrived there in due course. The survivors who reached Jamaica were diminished by

wrecked, and the two next vessels sent to their
succour arrived two months after the desertion of
the colony. These two ships brought about three
hundred men in addition to supplies, but one of the
ships was burnt a day or two after its arrival, and
the other, with both crews, excepting about six men,
who elected to remain with the Indians, sailed for
Jamaica, subsequently losing the greater part of
their number there.

The expedition to which the Rev. Francis Boreland was attached, set sail from Rothesay on Sept.
24, 1699. They were in all four ships, the "Rising
Sun," the "Companies' Hope" (on board which was
Mr. Boreland), the "Hamilton," and the "Hope,"
and the men on board, all told, numbered about 1,200.
The first land they made was the Island of Mont-
serrat, which they reached in six or seven weeks;
but the governor of the island, in accordance with
instructions received from England, denied them
water or provisions, and they moreover heard vague
rumours of the disasters which had attended the
first expedition, but they would not believe them.
Disaster attended this expedition as well as the
others—about one hundred and sixty having been
buried at sea—and the survivors arrived at Caledonia
to find nothing but a waste and howling wilderness.
"They looked for peace, but no good came; and for
a time of health and comfort, but behold trouble."
They were all the more discouraged because their

expedition was fitted out, not to settle a colony, but to recruit and supply a colony already settled and in working order. They fortunately found on their arrival two small sloops which had been sent with provisions from North America. One of the sloops was commanded by the Captain Drummond already alluded to. He had been a leading man in the first expedition, and had gone for supplies, with which he now waited the coming of the second expedition, and gave them an account of the first disaster.

The disasters had been so rapidly successive, that the leaders knew not how to act; and in the absence of instructions from Scotland, and till such had been received, they resolved to hold on to the colony; but in order to do so, they at first resolved to send off about five hundred of the colonists to Jamaica, and put the remaining members of the expedition on short allowance of provisions. The ships which were to carry these superabundant colonists were unable to get out of the harbour, owing to the winds, and on the arrival shortly after of Captain Campbell, of Finab, in a sloop from Barbadoes, with orders from home and some provisions, their despatch was countermanded, and a bold policy as regards the Spaniards was resolved on. Numerous skirmishes took place with the Spaniards both by sea and by land, but in the end the place was invested and the harbour blockaded. Water got scarce owing to the wells they dug in the fort affording "brackish and

Boreland, who was the only one of the ministers sent out to the colony who returned home; and from some time having elapsed between the events and the publishing the book, the narrative is apparently free from prejudice, and is the result of mature reflection.   His description of the country might in many respects serve for the present time.   He describes the natives as being almost without clothes, but contented with their state and thoughtless about the morrow; their houses as being mean, open at the sides, and only covered with plantain-leaves; the people as sleeping in hammocks made out of indigenous cotton.   They are said to be a slothful people, cultivating little patches surrounded with dense woods, which like a high wall encompass them about so that they may be justly said to be "like an owl in the desert, and the pelican in the wilderness." They do indeed, he says, inhabit the dark places of the earth.   Their food is said to be plantains (from which they also make drink), bananas, potatoes, yams, etc., and their religion, possibly, as far as he says he could make out, was the worship of the devil. The men, he says, hunt, and the women cook and do all the drudgery, both domestic and in the fields.

After quoting the experience of previous travellers and geographers regarding the unhealthiness of the country, he says that Peter Martyr, writing in 1514, describes the air of Darien as more pestiferous than that of Sardis: " the Spanish inhabitants are all pale and yellow like them that have the jaundice, and the nature of the soil being compassed about with muddy and stinking marshes, the infection whereof is much increased by the heat, their habitation, therefore, in Darien is pernicious, unwholesome, and contagious." Mr. Boreland remarks on this point, that it may be said of Darien, "Thou land devourest men and eatest up thy inhabitants." "No wonder, then, though our colony neither did nor could thrive there, suppose no other enemy in the world had molested them."

Of the first expedition he only speaks from hearsay, as the one to which he was attached did not set sail from the Clyde for three months after the first expedition had deserted the settlement. From one of the surviving counsellors, Captain Thomas Drummond, and from other sources, he learned that before they left they were so weakened by death and disease, that they could scarce find men to do sentry duty, and almost all were demoralized, and worn out by the dread of attacks from the neighbouring Spanish garrisons, with the fear of which they were daily alarmed by their friendly Indian neighbours.

There were also divided counsels among them, and though they had been seven months in Darien no letter had reached them from Scotland, and they were unaware of any relief or supplies being on the way; the first vessel sent from the Clyde with stores and reinforcements, in January 1699, was ship-

desertion, and at least one hundred more deaths took place, intemperance having hastened the end of many. The Rev. Mr. Shields, one of the most esteemed of the ministers, died in Jamaica, and two students in divinity attached to the expedition, besides Mr. James Main, the interpreter, who had drawn up the articles of capitulation. At last the remaining ships were re-fitted, and set sail for Scotland with their shattered crews. The chief ship, the " Rising Sun," with about one hundred and forty passengers and crew, soon got into trouble, and arrived dismasted off Charleston, N.C. There about fifteen of them, including the Rev. Mr. Stobo and his wife, landed, the large vessel not being able to get over the bar. During the night a hurricane came on which wrecked the ship, and all on board perished. Mr. Stobo remained as minister of a church in Charleston, and Mr. Boreland, the author of the very rare book I quote from, left the west of Jamaica, where the fleet had arrived for Port Royal; from thence he sailed to Boston, and so home by way of London.

The character of the colonists sent out, judging from the accounts given of them by the ministers who were sent with them, was very bad indeed; and the three surviving ministers sent with the second expedition, one having died on the voyage out, in writing to the moderator of the General Assembly, giving an account of the state of affairs,

the letter being dated "From the Woods of Caledonia, Feb. 2, 1700," says "the fountain cause of
all their miseries was brought from Scotland with
them, choice having been made of the scum of
the country, who were without the commonest
measures of religion or reason, honesty or honour,
and the conduct of the colonists, even on the voyage
out, being bad beyond belief," and, "since their
landing, such as threatens the final and fatal ruin of
the colony, to the irreparable loss and indelible
shame and reproach of the nation."

The voyage, and their experience on landing,
dispelled all dreams the ministers had of establishing
parishes and Presbyterian government ; and they
plaintively say that the church of New Edinburgh,
to which they had been sent, never had an existence,
and that among their number there was little chance
of finding any fit to form a session out of. They say
that one third of their number were "wild High-
landers that cannot speak or understand Scotch."
The Indians, they say, they could do no good to,
owing to their ignorance of each other's tongue ; but
these latter seem to have attended the religious
services notwithstanding, and at any rate appeared
to have listened silently and decorously. One of the
ministers, the Rev. Mr. Shields, who died in Jamaica,
according to Mr. Boreland, testified that he had been
in all parts of the world, and had served as a minister
with the army in Flanders, but that he had never

France, and that very little would induce the Scots' nobility to accept "the general commands, marechal staffs, ducal coronets, and annual pensions which their ancestors formerly had." Philo-Caledon's book called forth a spirited reply by "Philo-Briton," who, as the title-page has it, deals with the defence of the Scots' settlement "paragraph by paragraph." This description on the title-page is literally correct, as each paragraph of the defence is given and then answered, but always in a supercilious and over-bearing manner. Philo-Briton expresses the belief that England, which had twice been instrumental in breaking the chains of Europe, and thereby keeping up the balance of power and the repose of the continent without the assistance of the Scots, would be able to maintain its ancient glory without their new settlement in Darien. He sarcastically thanks the author, Philo-Caledon, for his kindness in easing England of the Scotch pedlars. He, however, expresses the fear, that if they were permitted to furnish silks, muslins, etc., from the East by way of Darien, they would all turn wholesale men, and, instead of carrying a pack on their back, would invest in pack-horses and intensify the evil.

The collapse of the scheme was of momentous importance to the history of Scotland and England as regards their separate interests and their relations to each other. When the fact of the bursting of their great national scheme and of their first expedition was with great difficulty brought home to the Scotch, a storm of indignation was raised which the King's high commissioner was at his wit's end to allay. The local authorities were up in arms, and the chief shires and burgs all sent in protests and petitions declaring that the colony of Caledonia was a *legal settlement*, and as such must be supported. Numerous addresses were presented to the Scotch parliament and to the king, and the national feeling, as then understood, was thoroughly aroused. A petition and representation of the company to the high commissioner and estates of parliament, dated 28th October 1700, stated that nothing having been done regarding previous representations, they had now to report that their worst anticipations were realised, and that, owing to the active steps taken by his majestic's allies, the King of Spain and the Governor of Carthagena, the colonists had, to the dishonour of the nation, surrendered their settlement ; and that the proclamations from the colonial governments being still in force, they could not even carry off their ships lying perishing at Port Royal, Jamaica, Ambey Perth, N. J.; and that the Governor of Jamaica had declared that he would not give up the company's ship "S. Andrew," without a special warrant from England. The Duke of Queensbury, the high commissioner, fenced with the question and adjourned the meeting of the Scots' parliament for three weeks. He said, according to a broadside which I have, that "he had such a cold

his own act of parliament in Scotland establishing
the company, and also to the interest of the nation.
As they are the act of a person who is really King of
Scots, the only inference is that they are the effect
of force put upon him, and that the King of Scots is
detained in England and not master of himself.
The condition of Scotland, as matters are, the writer
says, " is worse than that of a foreigner who has his
own king to appeal to, whereas the Scotchman has
none if his interest clashes with England. If he is
inclinable to do justice as King of the Scots, he finds
himself a prisoner in England and cannot do it."
All kinds of arguments are used to disarm English
opposition, and it is pointed out that there ought to
be no jealousy, as no special advantages are claimed
by the Scots for themselves.

One argument is, that if the colony went on, the
Scots would increase their shipping, and come in
time to have a naval force capable of assisting the
English in the common defence of the island. Their
wealth would also increase, and so enable them to
bear a share of any foreign war both in men and
money. Another argument is, that England was
the seat of government ; the wealth acquired in trade
would be spent there, and vast sums would be spent
in London by the nobility and gentry. Another
argument which seems to have been thought a very
weighty one, is used by Philo-Caledon. He says
that the success of the Scots in their foreign planta-

tion will not only ease England of great numbers of
their pedlars, so frequently complained of in parliament by country corporations and shopkeepers, but
it will occasion the return home and prevent the
going out of vast numbers of their youth who follow
the same sort of employment, or betake themselves
to the sword in Denmark, Sweden, Poland, Muscovy,
Germany, Holland, and France ; by which means the
government of Great Britain may furnish their fleets
and armies at a much easier and cheaper rate than
formerly, and with as good mariners and soldiers as
any in the world.

In a book entitled " Vindication of Darien," published in the same year, which copy I bought at
the sale of Dr. Laing (and in his handwriting on the
title-page is ascribed to William Paterson himself),
many of the same arguments are used. He says
that though he would hope no provocation would
drive them to the step, nothing would be more
natural than that, as with individuals unkindly
treated by their friends, the Scots should seek succour and relief wherever they could obtain it. The
Dutch, he says, if appealed to, would gladly espouse
their cause ; and the French, with whom the Scots
had more affinity than with any other nation, had
not forgotten the benefits which had redounded to
each other's benefit in the past. He says that the
brave soldiers furnished to France by Scotland were
mainly instrumental in driving the English out of

been mixed up with such a company before; and Mr. Stobo, writing from Charleston after his settlement there, said "they were such a rude company, that Sodom never declared such impudence in sinning as they."

Mr. Boreland finished his calm and dispassioned account in verse, which is very much to the point, if not of a very high character:—

> " No wonder, then, our infant colony
> In Darien could not long time thriving be,
> By such ill neighbours in a spot of earth
> Beset with griefs, and daily views of death,
> Remote from friends, the objects of envy
> To many, who did wish we here might die ;
> Our single strength but feeble to support us ;
> Our skill in such affairs small to direct us ;
> Besides an higher cause of our distresses,
> God's wrath against us, for our great trespasses.
> Then strange not that our new plantation
> Soon died and came to desolation."

In " Æsop in Scotland," a collection of fables published in London in 1704, and of which I have a copy, there is one fable entitled "The Merchants and Soldiers" which holds up the expedition to ridicule in rather easier rhymes than the foregoing :—

> " In a country north where the winds they are nipping,
> Where money is scarce, as well as good shipping,
> Where ill-natured people are always inventing,
> Grand knavish intrigues and as often repenting ;
> A mighty projection came into their noddles,
> To ride a long journey with bridles and saddles.

In a place in the Indies they thought to be masters,
But soldiers and merchants met woful disasters;
For want of good vituals, good soldiers and treasure,
They were forced to return without profit or pleasure;
The merchants were ready to die with vexation,
Because 'twas a baulk to their antient great nation.
Such a voyage, say the soldiers, was ne'er undertaken,
For instead of gold-dust we have lost all our bacou.
We thought to be great, but the Deil take the loons,
They almost stripped off the skin from our bones;
Like ghosts we returned upon our own coast,
And therefore we have little cause for to boast;
No moral for this, for the case it is plain,
These soldiers will hardly go thither again."

An interesting account of Darien was written in 1699 by Philo-Caledon, who also defends the legality of the Scots' settlement there, and, in writing against the Spanish memorial against it, tries to show that it is the interest of England to join with the Scots to maintain and protect it. The writer argues that if the English continue to enforce the proclamation issued against the Darien Expedition, the Scotch may be thrown into the arms of the French, to whom they could at any time honourably capitulate, renew their ancient alliance, and recover all their special privileges. In return for the nominal surrender of their sovereignty they might have all the benefits derivable from the Darien trade, and uninterrupted enjoyment of their religion. He points out that the English proclamations in the West Indies cannot be the act and deed of a king of Scotland, since they are diametrically opposed to

and hoarseness " that he could no longer stay. He protested his faithfulness to his king and his native land, and declared that he had the king's full instructions for everything that would advantage the nation and particularly benefit the African and Indian company; but that, all things considered, he thought he had better consult his majesty in person. Evidently he was fairly overcome by the outcry, and was very glad of an excuse to get away from his indignant fellow-countryman, and so save controversy which might have made matters worse.

The extent to which the nation would have been carried in consequence of its wounded pride and money losses when the worst was finally known, would have doubtless ended in an armed outbreak, but for the dread of still greater troubles. The sufferers from the failure of the scheme were almost entirely low-land Scotch, and these chiefly the inhabitants of the towns, who were, to a man, supporters of the revolution of 1688, and therefore devoted to King William. They were moreover inspired with a dread of the return of the Stewarts with whom they associated popery, prelacy, persecution, and subserviency to France. The northern half of the kingdom had no such feeling ; as a rule their sympathies were the reverse ; and the Darien sufferers were constrained to restrain their feelings and abstain from violence, in which, had they indulged, they would have found no want of sympathisers and willing abettors. There

was a great disposition shewn to exonerate the king
from the blame of the breakdown of the scheme, and
the language of the author of " An humble Address
to the Scots' Parliament" expresses the situation
when he speaks of the king as being the nursing
father of the church and nation, and appeals to him
" to send an olive branch of an answer of peace to
their cry, and to aid in sending blessings and prosperity to this distressed and impoverished nation."

The addresses and petition presented to the king
directly and through his high commissioners were
very numerous, and shewed a spirit which must have
convinced the king that the company and the nation
were in earnest. These addresses are too long to
go much into, but in July 1700, from his court at
Loo, the king wrote that he was deeply sensible of the
losses of the company, and "being heartily inclined
to advance the wealth and prosperity" of his ancient
kingdom of Scotland, he promised to concur with
his parliament in everything that would support their
interests and repair their losses. He promised also
to protect his said ancient kingdom from all their
enemies, and trusted that in return they would not
suffer themselves to be misled, and so give an advantage to enemies and ill-designing persons.

In the earlier period of the year, in reply to an
address from the House of Lords, the king spoke of
the way in which he had been touched by the losses his
kingdom of Scotland had sustained—a kingdom for

E

which he had "a great concern and tenderness:"
" His majesty does apprehend that difficulties may
too often arise with respect to the different interests
of trade between the two kingdoms, unless some way
be found to unite them more nearly and completely."
He reminds them, therefore, of his recommendation
to his parliament soon after his accession—" that
they should consider of an union between the two
kingdoms." Such an union, he says, would con-
tribute to the security and happiness of the two
kingdoms; and he adds a hope that "after they had
lived one hundred years under one king some happy
expedient might be found for making them one
people."

In April 1702, Queen Anne acknowledges an
address from the parliament of Scotland, which, she
says, would have been answered by her predecessor
had not death prevented. In it she intimates her
firm purpose to maintain the sovereignty and independency of her ancient kingdom against all invasions
and encroachments, and promises to be equally
tender of the rights, prerogatives, and liberties of
the crown and kingdom of Scotland as of those of
England, and says her chief design would be to
govern both according to their respective laws and
liberties, and to avoid all occasions of misunder-
standing or difference; adding, "and for this end
we shall think it our happiness to establish an
entire union between the two kingdoms upon an

equal and just foundation, and the parliament of our kingdom of England having shewn so good an inclination to this union, we expect that nothing on your part will obstruct a design so useful for the happiness of both kingdoms."

In this proclamation she further promises that no Scotsmen shall be impressed for sea-service in the English fleet ; regrets the losses incurred through the Darien Expedition, and promises to back up any project for their reparation and assistance. The reparation came at last in what was called " The Equivalent." A short explanation of this term and of what led up to it is necessary. The discussions regarding the union between the two kingdoms were very prolonged, and often of a very angry character. The spirit which had been roused in Scotchmen over their treatment by the English in their late efforts after foreign trade was as bitter as ever, and was liable to break out into flames at any moment. One episode which shewed this feeling occurred in April 1705. Captain Green, the commander of the English East Indiaman, the "Worcester," having had by stress of weather to put into the Forth, was seized by the authorities in retaliation for a seizure in the Thames of a ship of the South African Company. Some of the crew charged Green with the seizure of a Scotch vessel in the East Indies, and with the murder of the captain (Drummond) and the crew. Green was tried for murder and piracy, and with his first officer and gunner was executed, though professing entire ignorance of the Scotch ship's existence. The populace was furious against these men, and the news of their death aroused equally violent feeling in England, and extreme retaliatory measures were proposed. Better councils, however, prevailed. Negotiations were continued, and the leaders of both sides saw the absolute necessity of an arrangement being come to. The chief difficulty lay in the arranging as regards the incidence of taxation and trade questions generally.

Finally, in arranging a scheme of union, it was conceded that the Scots were prejudiced to the extent of £398,085 by duties and customs they were called to bear in consequence of their assuming their share of the debts of England. This amount was called "The Equivalent," and from it her majesty was empowered to pay the national debt of Scotland and the Darien capital stock with interest. The balance was to be used in payments of loss in the Scotch currency, and for encouraging the fisheries and manufactures of the country.

A committee was appointed to report on the affairs of the Indian and African Company, and the result was that they found the total stock advanced by the proprietors, with interest at five per cent to the 1st May 1707, amounted to £229,482. 15s. 1d. sterling, and that the total debts of the company amounted to £14,809. 18s. 11d. sterling, both sums amounting to

£244,292. 14s. From this sum several proprietors
had borrowed about £1,126, so that the real amount
of capital and debts was £243,166. They recom-
mended that Gavin Plummer and Andrew Cockburn,
the late company's cashiers, should be empowered to
receive the same amount from the Commissioners of
the Equivalent, and act as cashiers and tellers for its
distribution. A balance of £1,654, expected to be
realised from the sale of the ship "Caledonia," lying
in the Clyde, the wrecked ship "Speedwell," in the
East Indies, the Edinburgh warehouse in Milne
Square, and sundry other items, was to be used for
office expenses during distribution of the Equivalent,
and to enable the council and directors to pay "such
necessary allowances and satisfaction to the several
gentlemen who had suffered in their persons and
goods as their cases may warrant."

This arrangement was proclaimed from the Market
Cross of Edinburgh, in August 1707, and thus ended
the African Company.

Paterson's connection with the expedition itself
seems to have been slight, though at a meeting of
the board, in 1696, he was appointed to go with
other two directors, to engage foreign merchants,
and to negotiate regarding trade generally. Till
some time after sailing he was not a member of
council, and he seems to have had no influence
during the voyage. On his return home, in December
1699, he addressed a report to the directors, and

in it complains that when he suggested a meeting of
council before sailing, "so that the commanders might
rectify any omission in their stores," he was told in
plain language to mind his own business. His story,
as told in his report, is a melancholy record of divided
counsels, jealousies, and bitter altercations. Paterson
says that on the 5th June 1699, he was taken ill of
a fever, "but trouble of mind was none the least
cause thereof." Ten days after, he was carried on
board the "Unicorn," which ship, along with the
"S. Andrew" and "Caledonia," conveyed the survivors of the first expedition. His journey was a
most disastrous one, and it was a wonder he recovered.
He states that one hundred and fifty out of the two
hundred and fifty who embarked with him at Darien,
died before they reached New York, on the 13th
August 1699. They died, he says, "mostly from
want of looking after and means to recover them."
His indisposition was such that he was incapacitated
from taking any further part in the expedition, and
two months afterwards he sailed from New York for
home, arriving in Islay in about a month. After
some delay he crossed to the mainland, and, owing
to the state of his health, travelled by easy stages to
Edinburgh, arriving there in about a fortnight,
broken down in health and spirits by the sad experi-
ences of the eighteen months that had elapsed since
his sailing from Leith.

Paterson's activity of mind returned with the

return of health, and documents preserved in the
British Museum show that but for the untimely death
of King William, the latter might have been won
over to Paterson's scheme as an important factor
in his opposition to France and Spain. Paterson
wrote largely on political economy and kindred
subjects, and passed the remainder of his life chiefly
in the literary and political circles of London. He
died in 1718, and his will was proved for some £7,000.

An attempt to compensate him for his losses was
made in his later years by the House of Commons,
which passed a bill granting him £18,400, but it was
thrown out by the House of Lords, and nothing more
was done in the matter.

The contemporary pamphlets and books relating
to the Scotch Darien Expedition are generally very
roughly printed on inferior paper, but such is the
interest in the subject, that the prices they command
must seem absurd to those who have not taken an
interest in the subject, and who are not, to some
extent, bibliomaniacs.